Email Marketing for Authors Made Simple: The 1-Page List Building Plan

This book was written by Anita Nipane of Digginet.

Copyright © 2020 by Anita Nipane.
All rights reserved. No part of this book may be used or reproduced in any manner whatsoever without written permission except in the case of brief quotations embodied in critical articles or reviews.

Trademarks
All product and brand names identified throughout this book are used for their benefit with no intention of infringement of their copyrights.

Affiliate Disclosure
This book contains affiliate links. If you use these links to buy something, the author may earn a commission.

For more information, contact:
http://www.digginet.com

First Edition: November 2020

Contents

Why Build Your Email List? 5

Build Your Email Marketing Ecosystem 7

    A Funnel Book 9

        How to Make Your Book Perma-free on Amazon? 14

    In-Book Reader Magnet 16

        7 Ideas for Highly-Converting Reader Magnets for Nonfiction Authors 18

        3 Ideas for Creative Reader Magnets for Fiction Authors 21

        Opt-in Form 23

3 Author-friendly Tactics to Build Email List 25

    Cross Promotions 25

    Joint Promotions 31

    Giveaways 37

Plan Your Email Content Calendar 42

    Nurture Your Readers with Automated Email Sequences 44

    Welcome Email Sequence 46

    Reviewer Sequence 51

    Launch Team Sequence 53

    Re-engagement Sequence 55

    Broadcast emails 59

Segment Your Email List 63

    How to Group Your Contacts? 67

        Email Lists 68

        Tagging 69

The Art of Writing Catchy Subject Lines 72

Measure Your Email Performance 77

5 Questions to Answer Before Choosing Your Email Marketing Platform.83

Now it's your turn!..88

Found a Typo?...90

Other Books by the Author 91

About the Author..93

Why Build Your Email List?

The harsh truth is – the author with the biggest and most loyal email list wins. It means as long as you have an email list, you can literally launch any book and be sure that it will be profitable.

No other audience, be it on the blog or any social media platform, will be as responsive as your email subscribers will. If you have a big email list, you can reach more eyeballs, get more sales, receive more reviews, and earn better Amazon sales ranks. What's more, thanks to regular communication with your email subscribers, you know their usual response rate and interests. Therefore, you can predict your free and paid book download numbers, income, and even book rankings to some degree. It means you do not have to rely on hope anymore.

Why? Because you can send out an email and generate instant and targeted traffic to any piece of content you choose – be it a blog post, a YouTube video, or your book on Amazon. You do not have to buy ads or work on SEO to achieve the result (although it is also important). Your only expense is the fixed monthly cost of your email marketing platform. In addition, it does not matter if you send one email campaign a month or ten, because the cost doesn't increase. After a small initial investment to get an email address, you never have to pay for that traffic again. Whereas if you use paid advertising, every additional reach and click costs you more money.

Nevertheless, with the tactics I'm going to show you in this book, you can build your author email list even for free and with no initial investment at all. So, let's move to the next chapter!

Build Your Email Marketing Ecosystem

Do you really need a blog or author website? The short answer is no. You can publish your books on Amazon and be quite successful even if you do not have a website. However, you definitely need an email-marketing ecosystem that consists of a landing page, a lead magnet, subscription forms, and a communication plan.

A simple landing page can be a good place start, but building an author platform should be the next step for every self-published author who wants to scale in the long-term.

Why? Because thanks to your author platform, you can build your brand, communicate your expertise, increase credibility and bring in organic traffic that will help you build your email list and cut down on your marketing costs. Additionally, in case Amazon changes the rules or you simply want to become more independent, you have your own audience and options to sell to them directly.

Whatever decision you make concerning your self-publishing journey, the most important thing is to have a long-term vision and goal in mind. That way, you will be able to choose the best tools, tactics, and strategies for you.

To help you make a well-considered decision, in this book I'll give you an insight into the purpose and usage of the main elements of an efficient author email marketing ecosystem. Because that is exactly what it is about – you need to build your system.

A Funnel Book

If you have read my book, "5 Secret Strategies of Kindle Publishing: Earn Passive Income with Nonfiction Books," you should already be familiar with the concept of book series strategy. In short, the idea here is that you must focus on one niche only and publish your book in a series of 3 to 5 books that are targeted to a specific audience. This way, you will build your readership in the same market and will be able to focus all your marketing efforts on reaching the audience in your chosen niche.

Moreover, each book in your series should link to the entire series so that when readers click on the description of one of your books, they will see all of them, like in the example below. This is a distraction-free page that shows only your books, which makes it a great landing page to link to from your website or social media because you won't promote other authors' books.

The goal of your first book of the series is to hook your readers. So, make it exceptional. Do not include all your content in the first book. Save some of it for your next books. Make it clear to readers that the book is a part of a series. Mention your other books (if you have or are going to have them) and include links to them. Then **make this book perma-free on Amazon** and give it away on your web page or landing page in exchange for email addresses. This is your Funnel Book, and its goal is to help you to grow your audience and email list.

What is a Funnel Book? It is a book that introduces your target audience to your topic, ideas, writing style, and author's brand. The goal of this book is to serve as the first step to entering your sales funnel so that you can segment out your loyal fans and email subscribers. It is important that this book works on its own. The reader of your Funnel Book should find it so useful (and be so grateful that it has solved their problem) that they will be keen to get your other books. If you write fiction, then your first book should end with cliffhangers to entice your readers to get the next book in the sequel and continue reading the story.

You may think that it's a clever idea to include only the first few chapters to make the reader want to buy your full book to get the remaining content, but this can boomerang terribly and make them resent you.

There are four advantages of having a Funnel Book:
- Making your Funnel Book as perma-free on Amazon helps you reach new audiences and readers that previously didn't even know you exist. They will find your free book on relevant categories, in Amazon lists, like, Books You May Like, and when doing a keyword search on Amazon. It is a huge potential you don't want to miss because, based on my experience, free books tend to have 10-1000 times more downloads than paid books (even than $ 0.99 books). As your Funnel Book, it will lead your readers to your other books on Amazon (if you have them) and will work as free advertising for you as an author.
- Offering the Funnel Book as a reader magnet on your web page helps you convert its visitors into targeted email subscribers that are interested in your topic and other books of the series.
- Use your Funnel Book to participate in joint promotions and giveaways, as well as to promote on free promotion sites and with Facebook ads if you are good at them. That way, you will leverage

your Funnel Book to the fullest because it will help you to both get more email subscribers and promote your other (paid) books to new audiences.

- Using your Funnel Book as a lead magnet gives you control over what content your email subscribers see and in what sequence. For example, if you know that all your email subscribers have downloaded your Funnel Book, you can offer them useful content that is not covered in this book and leads to your other books. It means you can easily automate your emails to provide valuable content in a logical sequence since you already know what they have read. For example, my Funnel Book is "5 Secret Strategies of Kindle Publishing: Earn Passive Income with Nonfiction Books," which is a great introduction to the topic of Kindle publishing. It is mostly targeted to aspiring and new self-published authors. Since I know the readers that have downloaded this book are interested in Kindle publishing, I know exactly what content to offer them in my emails and other books to lead them through my sales funnel.

If you have several book series for different audiences, it may make sense to have perma-free Funnel Books for each of them. Just remember to segment your audiences when you are creating your email campaigns. You will read how to do this in one of the next chapters.

Some authors are concerned about making their books free, as those types of books only attract a certain type of reader, namely freebie seekers. And this might be partly true. However, there is a trick to it. If you can get people into your work and hook them with your experience and knowledge (non-fiction) and storytelling and plots (fiction), you can convert your free book reader to a paying customer. The goal of your Funnel Book is to work like the doorway to your other books, services, and products. If the Funnel Book does do its job, you'll find people buying and reading the next book, and then all your other books in the series.

If the book doesn't do its job, then the worst that may happen is you have a reader who won't buy full-price books. However, thanks to their downloads, your book ranking will increase, and you will have a better chance to reach more eyeballs and paying readers.

How to Make Your Book Perma-free on Amazon?

So, by now, you may have a question... how to make your book perma-free on Amazon? You won't find such an option on your KDP setup page. The lowest price Amazon accepts is $0.99. You cannot directly set the price of your book to free or $0.00. The only way to make your book perma-free on Amazon is to first list it somewhere else as free and then request that Amazon price match to the free copy on the other site.

These are the steps you must take to **make your book perma-free on Amazon**:

1. When you are publishing your book on Amazon, price it at $0.99 and DON'T enroll in KDP Select.
2. Sign up for a service like Smashwords or Draft2Digital. These platforms will let you publish your book on many other book retailers, like Barnes & Noble, iBooks, Kobo, and others.
3. You may want to customize your book manuscript to remove Amazon links because some of the competing online bookstores (for example, Apple) do not want to promote Amazon and will reject your book. However, other sites like Kobo, Scribd, and Barnes & Noble may allow them. Then publish your book with the price at $0.00.
4. Once your book is listed for free on Barnes and Noble or Apple's iBooks, log in to your KDP dashboard and send a note to KDP Support. In your KDP Account, select "Help" and "Contact Us." Then under the "Pricing" section, select "Price Matching" and tell

Amazon that your book is available for free on these other bookstores. Provide them with the links to the retailers where your book is free and kindly request that they match that price of $0 on Amazon, as well.

5. Wait for a response from Amazon. Usually, it takes around 24 – 48 hours for the book to be made perma-free.

If after some time you want to price your book again, you can easily do that. Simply go to your KDP dashboard and increase your book's price to whatever number you want.

In-Book Reader Magnet

A reader magnet (also known as a lead magnet, freemium, incentive, etc.) is one more crucial part of an email marketing ecosystem. Its goal is to draw your most interested audience into your email list. Reader magnets are nothing new and are widely used in different markets because of how persuasive and powerful they can be.

In case you don't know, a reader magnet is a piece of valuable information that you give away for free in exchange for readers signing up to your mailing list. It must be something exciting that tempts readers to fill out a subscription form because people are not usually willing to give out their email addresses.

I will give you a few reader magnet ideas a little bit later in this book, but for now, think about what information would be juicy enough for people to want to exchange emails with you. Consider that the reader magnet should do exactly what the name implies – attract readers to your newsletter and your connected series. In order to create a good one, you must know your target audience very well and offer something that is connected to your book topic.

Why do you need to spend your time creating an additional reader magnet if you already have the perma-free book?

Because someone might read your book and like it, but when the reading is finished, he moves on to another book and forgets about you. Offering a reader magnet in your book is the only way you can convert your anonymous Amazon readers into trackable and easily approachable email subscribers. If you regularly collect the email addresses of your book readers, you'll gradually build up a list of targeted audience that you know already enjoy your writing.

Moreover, if you use a unique reader magnet for each book that is accessible only for its readers, every time someone subscribes for this reader magnet, it will be a sign that this person owns the particular book and probably have read and enjoyed it. That is your chance to create an automated email sequence with a kind request to leave a review for your book on Amazon or whatever online bookstore you publish on. That way, you will start getting reviews on autopilot.

7 Ideas for Highly-Converting Reader Magnets for Nonfiction Authors

When a reader picks up a nonfiction book, it usually means they want to learn something and are open to new information. Therefore, an additional free content piece can feel like a good deal to them. In general, an ideal reader magnet should solve a specific problem for your target audience and inspire transformation by providing actionable steps. It should be something practical and easily consumable.

A good way to find ideas for your reader magnet topic is to look for what people are already paying for. That might sound counterintuitive because reader magnets are free. However, if someone is willing to part with their money to get particular information, it is a sure sign that they are passionate about the topic.

So, where to find those ideas? Simply head on to the resource you are already familiar with – the Kindle Store. Go through your niche categories and subcategories and look at the bestselling books in each of them to find common trends and catchy titles you can transform into a content piece for your reader magnet. Look at their tables of content and read reviews to see what readers liked or disliked about the books. Do not copy or plagiarize but get inspired and generate your own ideas.

When you have decided on your reader magnet topic, it's time to choose its format. Below are listed some of the most popular ones.

1. Checklist

If you write instructional books, you can easily transform them into checklists. All you have to do is summarize the book content into a list of bullet points, and you are ready to go. If you need inspiration, go through the checklist templates in Checkli.com and then use Canva templates to create a beautiful design and export it as a PDF or JPG file to make it printable and easy to use. That way, your readers can print the file and cross off the list as they work through it. This gives them a physical sense of achievement as they go about their lives and business.

2. Cheat Sheet

If your book talks about a complicated and complex subject matter, it is a very good idea to give your readers a shortcut or a cheat sheet guide on how to navigate that subject. Again, simply go through your book's main points and summarize them in a logical sequence. This can be a great resource your readers can easily refer to in order to refresh their memories when they get confused. It takes a lot of pressure off readers because they do not have to remember every single step to implement your strategies. Make your cheat sheet in a very compact and printable format that readers can easily glance through and understand.

3. Swipe File

A swipe file is a compilation of templates and different resources that your reader might refer back to later. These can be email copies, blog post titles, sales letters, ad templates, video scripts, and many other useful resources. There is an overabundance of valuable information available on the Internet, and people would be grateful if they can get a compiled and very practical version of it and save their time. Moreover, swipe files can be very useful for you, too.

If you're anything like me, you have a folder on your computer that contains swipe-able email and blog post titles. Maybe you even have a subfolder in your email inbox with marketing emails from other people in your industry that inspire you when you are writing promotional emails to your audience. By the way, this is a great, free resource full of swipe files that you can use for inspiration: https://swiped.co/.

If you're not like me, then you probably should be. Become obsessed with your niche, and you will be surprised at what you can learn by following the best marketing content examples from your industry experts! Moreover, you can transform your swipe files into effective reader magnets and exchange them for email addresses or even sell them as a digital product.

4. Resource Guide
A resource guide is very easy to create. The idea of this lead magnet is that you recommend resources and tools that can save your audience time and money. This guide can be a collection of anything and everything that will help them achieve the results they want to achieve.

5. Email Course
The advantage of an email course is that you can segment the information you want to give into smaller chunks and send them to your prospects via automated email sequence. With this approach, your email subscribers

will get used to receiving emails from you and you will build a stronger relationship with them.

6. Instructional Video

A "how-to" video that explains the topic you are covering in your book more deeply or introduces the topic of the next book can work as a great reader magnet. Use practical examples to illustrate your idea and provide step-by-step instructions for achieving the result. This should be a short (up to 30 minutes) video. If you feel comfortable on camera, you can do a talking-head video, or simply show slides on your computer, or record your screen if you need to navigate the web or software.

7. Book

Your reader magnet can also be a free book that is available exclusively only via a subscription link that you place in your books. Of course, spending a lot of time writing a good quality book you will give away for free may not sound appealing to somebody (including me). However, it can still be a good tactic to hook your loyal readers.

3 Ideas for Creative Reader Magnets for Fiction Authors

1. **Chapter upgrades**

Write a short scene that describes the point of view of one of your book's characters. Or provide a picture of what character X is doing while the scene in the book is happening or tell a short backstory that is related to the places mentioned in your book. Offer this as a content upgrade in exchange for the reader's email address by placing a link at the end of the chapter or any other book part.

2. Personality quizzes

Personality quizzes like "What Game of Thrones character are you?" and similar are getting more and more popular. Come up with some funny and entertaining quiz that is related to your book story or its characters. Ask fun and easy to answer questions in your quiz and request participants' email addresses to send the results to their inbox.

3. Your next book's first chapter

One of the easiest options that don't require additional work is to offer the first chapter of your next book as your reader magnet. It is a good way to introduce readers to your next story and let them have a taste of your storytelling and writing skills.

To wrap it up, I don't suggest you create many different reader magnets for the same niche because in order to do it right, you will need to create welcome emails and implement tagging systems and auto-responder sequences for each of them to build a targeted and personal communication. In addition, all this stuff takes time and energy you could spend on more useful and entertaining things. It is not about offering as many reader magnets as possible. Rather, it is about implementing a system that is automated and trackable so that you can easily analyze the results and make improvements.

How to promote your reader magnet?

Usually, reader magnets are placed in the introductory chapter and closing part of the book. The introductory chapter works great if you also want to hook those Amazon surfers who only check your "look inside" section to know if the book is a good fit for them but won't eventually buy it. Moreover, the reality is – even many BUYERS will not read your book to the end for one reason or another. Maybe their toddler screams, a dog rings the bell to go out, or their spouse texts a message or anything else happens that distracts the readers and makes them forget about your book. That is why putting a big and bold advertisement in the introduction AND closing part of your book is the best way to be double sure your reader magnet will get noticed.

If your reader has made it to the end of your book, most probably, they enjoyed the content. Therefore, this is a good time to remind them about your incentive and ask them to subscribe to your email list. Present your offer as a free gift or a 'thank you' for reading the entire book. That way, you will have a list of your target audience when you are ready to launch your next book.

Opt-in Form

Often neglected, a simple newsletter subscription form can do wonders in terms of growing a list of very loyal and targeted email subscribers. If you don't offer any incentive, and readers still subscribe to your newsletter, it means they have found a hero in you and truly want to be notified about your upcoming books and other news. The bad news is the conversion rate of opt-in forms is much worse than that of incentivized reader magnets. However, simple sign-up links should still be a part of your email marketing ecosystem and placed in your book closing part and embedded in your website or landing page.

In case you write books for different market segments (for example, fiction and nonfiction,) ask your new contacts what kind of information they would want to receive when they sign up. Although interests may overlap in some cases, your fiction readers will most probably not be interested in your nonfiction books and vice versa. So, give them a chance to choose what content they want to receive.

3 Author-friendly Tactics to Build Email List

As you already know, one of the ways to collect email addresses is to include a link to a signup page in your books. Then you can expect that some of your readers will sign up for your reader magnet and become your email subscriber. However, unless your books sell in thousands of copies every day, this may be too slow a way to build your email list and may feel discouraging. If you do not have other sources of traffic to send people to your landing page, it may take forever to significantly grow your email list.

Therefore, in this chapter, I'll give you three author-friendly tactics to grow your email list quickly and almost for free.

Cross Promotions

So, how do authors use cross-promotions to grow their email lists? In short, they find another author that has a similar audience (in terms of topic and size), make friends with them, and then advertise each other's books to their email lists or on social media if they have a huge following. It is a mutually beneficial way to grow your audience, get new subscribers, and boost book sales.

Let's assume you write about dog training and have 1,000 subscribers on your list. All you need to do is approach another author in the same niche who also has about 1,000 subscribers on their list, and both of you will agree to email each other's freebies (usually Funnel Books) to your list. That way, you can both reach 1,000 new targeted readers in your niche. Let's assume about 10% of them convert. Each of you grows your email lists by 100 subscribers in a couple of days. Doesn't it sound great? No expensive paid ads, no other additional expenses. Moreover, it costs nothing to set up and get you measurable results fast.

You may be thinking: "But what to do if I'm starting from scratch and don't have 1,000 email subscribers or followers yet?" I'll give you some ideas in the next chapter. So, stay with me.

Another question you may have is: "Where to find authors in your niche to collaborate with and why would they agree?"

The answer is – Amazon. Go to your niche categories and click on the Top 100 Free Kindle books. Go through the list of books and their authors. Most probably, these are their Funnel Books, especially if they are offered as perma-free (for more than 5 days). Open the author's page and see if they have a website.

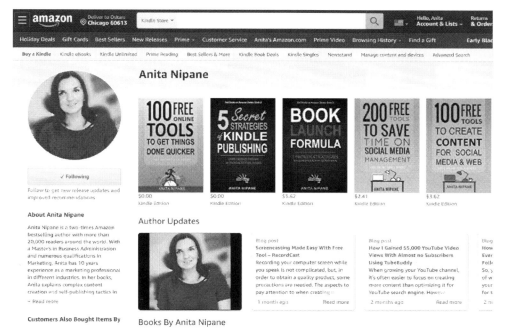

If yes, visit it and look for email subscription forms, which prove that the author collects email addresses and is active on their blog. There is no point in approaching somebody who published a book and then left the party.

Similarly, like with creating your customer avatar, you need to understand the avatar of your ideal cooperation partner. Who is this person? How many subscribers do they have on their list? Do their books have many positive reviews? How good are their book sales? You can easily get an idea by looking at their ABSRs.

All these are signs that show how committed these authors are to their publishing business and how big their audience might be. You need to understand that for many authors, book publishing is just a side hustle.

They may not be very motivated to work on growing their business. You can easily recognize these authors if you open their Amazon author pages and see that they have just a few books with a couple of reviews, weak ABSRs, and no website. Even if you search on Google, you will find nothing about these authors.

On the other hand, you will notice many authors with apparently huge audiences, great sales ranks, and beautiful webpages. Those authors are committed. Depending on how large your own audience is, you may decide who your ideal cooperation partner is. If you are just starting out, try to identify those who also are starting out and are committed. If you are an influencer yourself, approach other influencers in your niche.

It is what it sounds like! Do your homework and stalk your potential promotion partners at first – in a positive way. If they have a freebie on their website, download it and check its quality. Is it something worth your email? Do you want to suggest it to your fans? If no, move away and look for another partner. Be selective.

Wait, what happens when you subscribe to their newsletter? What kind of emails do you get? Do they send emails at all? If no, it may be a sign of inactivity.

Evaluate the potential audience of your promotion partner's website by using similarweb.com. If it shows huge numbers of website visitors, the author is most probably an influencer, and it might be very difficult to compel them to do a cross-promotion with you because their market power is much higher than yours. Of course, if you have tens of thousands of subscribers on your list, it would be the opposite, and approaching high-level influencers is the right choice for you. The key here is to be realistic on what you can offer to others and approach similar (or little bit above) level authors in terms of their audience size. If everything looks great, this is the time to make your move and address them.

Based on my experience, the best way to start communicating with an author who knows nothing about you is by replying to their email newsletter. If they are committed, they check their emails, and if they see that someone has replied to their newsletter, they will open and read it. And that's your goal – to make sure your email is opened and doesn't go unnoticed.

Moreover, since they are committed, they feel like the need to answer you because you are their subscriber. For example, I answer all emails I receive from my subscribers, but not all cold, general emails that offer some kind of cooperation because I do not feel like having any relationships with their senders.

When I use this tactic, I get about a 90% response rate. It doesn't mean they all want to collaborate with me, but still, I get a polite answer. In comparison, when I sent general emails that didn't indicate any connection with the receiver, I only got about a 15% response rate, and in 85% of cases, I got ignored.

Therefore, the conclusion is, you need to make your email sound personal. Reply to one of their newsletters and tell how much you love their blog posts or books and how you can help them promote their content if they are interested in doing a cross-promotion with you. Make it all about them. It works. Thanks to this tactic, I have done many joint promotions with authors who are complete strangers to me. Authors that previously didn't even know I existed. Sometimes we agree on cross-promoting each other's freebies; sometimes they may ask if I could promote their other piece of content or product. If it is mutually beneficial and would make sense to my audience, I take the deal!

The main advantage of doing cross-promotions, as opposed to joint promotions, is that you can control the quality of your partner's offer. Since you are the one who decides who to collaborate with, you can choose only those authors who write good quality content.

One more book promotion type is joint promotion. How does it differ from cross promotion? Read next.

Joint Promotions

The main difference between a joint promotion and a cross-promotion is that in this case, you team up with three or more other authors with similar audiences, and each participant promotes ALL the participants' books (instead of one at a time). That way, all promotion participants can significantly increase their reach.

Let's say you partner with ten other authors, and each of them has about 1,000 subscribers. They provide their free books to be placed on a landing page like the one below.

Searching for your next favorite story?

Look no further! These bestselling authors have teamed up to offer a delightful selection of new books. Available for a limited time.

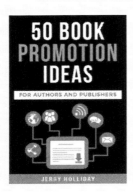  

When the promo starts, everybody invites their mailing list to check out the free books on the landing page. In order for a person to get these books, they need to join the authors' newsletters first. If all participants share the link to a free book offer page with their subscribers, you can reach 10,000 targeted readers.

That's a win-win strategy because thanks to the joint promotion, all participants can grow their email list.

Moreover, you can do joint promotions again and again, month after month, to keep a steady stream of new readers joining your list.

When the emails are collected, import them into your email marketing software (you can link your account to automate the process) to start communicating with your new fans. Remember to set up a welcome email sequence to greet all your new subscribers (more on that in one of the next chapters).

You may think - it's great if you already have partners that agree to do a joint promotion with you. But what to do if you don't? Luckily, there are online platforms that are built for this purpose and can help new book authors significantly grow their email lists.

Book promotion sites, like BookFunnel.com, BookBoast.com, MyBookCave.com, Storyorigin.com, ProlificWorks.com, BookSweeps.com, and TCKpublishing.com, provide a feature that allows authors to promote each other's free books to their email lists. They also have other useful features, like universal link building, simple landing page creation, and book delivery in multiple formats. But in this book, we will be discussing only the list-growing feature.

So, how does it work?
Simply sign up on any of these sites and add a book or books you'd like to give away for free to readers in exchange for their email addresses. Then join group promos where authors in a similar genre to yours gather. So, if

someone is running a giveaway for children's books, and you also have a children's book, you can join this group giveaway.

Usually, these promotions are free to join. However, some are paid, which means that you need to pay an entrance fee to join. For example, I pay $10 a month to participate in the BookFunnel promos that generate me hundreds of subscribers each month. No Facebook ad would do that for me for such a low price.

Of course, the success of this strategy is completely dependent on your niche, who your partners are, and the size of their list, but it's possible to add hundreds or even thousands of people to your list in just a few days using this strategy.

If you don't want to join any of the promotions that are available on these websites, you can organize your own joint promotions by creating a landing page and inviting other authors personally. A simple page with book images and links will do the job. I use GetResponse to create landing pages with a personalized domain name.

There are several advantages of organizing your own joint promotion:
- You can define the topic of the promotion according to the audience you want to reach. For example, you may want to partner with other authors who write about dog training, but there is no such option on book promotion sites.
- You can control who participates in the promotion. The disadvantage of book promotion sites is that low-quality books

are often submitted, or the books do not always correspond to the topic of the promotion. If you are not the organizer of the promotion, there's nothing you can do about this. Sometimes, I realize that the quality of other books in the promotion I joined is so low that I don't really want to share it with my subscribers. On the other hand, if I'm the organizer, I can weed out the irrelevant or low-quality books.

- You can also collaborate with authors who are not using book promotion sites. Why would you want to do that? Because after being on these websites for some time, I noticed that the audiences of the authors of the same genre often overlap since all of them use the same book promotion sites and do joint campaigns with the same authors all the time. For example, if the first campaigns gave me 300-400 new subscribers, then after a few months, I get only 50-70 new subscribers from a campaign. Actually, I get many more contacts, but half of them are duplicates, which means they are already on my list. It happens, especially if you use several free books for your promotions. Therefore, if after some time I want to reach a fresh audience that has not heard about me before, I need to collaborate with authors who are not on the book promotion sites.

- You can check the statistics of promotion participants to know what the potential of their mailing list is (for example, on BookFunnel). This information can be useful when you decide to do cross-promotions. Simply contact the authors who have a good list size (according to their data) and ask them if they would want to cooperate with you outside the promotion site. Over time, you'll build some great relationships you can use again and again to do cross-promotions also for your paid books and book launches.

However, the beauty of using book promotion websites, like BookFunnel and others, is that many of the promotions out there do not require a minimum mailing list size, which means you can join them with your free book **even if you have no mailing list or if it is very small**. Just be honest and share the information about the promotions you have joined on all the channels you can - be it your Facebook profile or five closest friends. When your email list grows bigger, your input into the success of the promotions will also get bigger.

Go into it with your eyes open. The subscribers you get from the promotions are cold. Most probably, they have not read your books previously. They only signed up because you gave them something for free. They may or may not ever read your free book. However, they may become loyal to you if you set up nurturing email automation sequences to warm them up and eventually convert them into paying readers.

Just remember that the free book you use in your promotions must be connected to your paid books and book series; otherwise, you will be attracting the wrong audience, and there will be no point having these emails on your list.

Giveaways

One of the quickest ways to build your email list is by doing a giveaway because thanks to this method, you can add thousands of new subscribers to your list very quickly. So, what is a giveaway and how does it differ from the two previous promotion types?

In short, during a giveaway, its entrants can win a prize in exchange for taking certain actions (i.e., subscribing to an email newsletter, sharing something on social media, answering a question, etc.). If you organize your giveaway to grow your email list, ask all entrants to provide their email addresses. You can also ask them to follow you on social media, comment on the giveaway post, answer a short poll, or do other activities. Just be aware that the more actions your potential subscriber needs to perform to enter your giveaway, the higher the possibility that they won't.

Let's start with choosing the prize for your giveaway. Your first idea might be to offer your own books as the prize. However, if you are a new author, getting people to care about your books will be very difficult. That's why you're running a giveaway, aren't you? The goal is to increase your readership. If you had a ton of loyal fans already, you wouldn't need to do giveaways to build your audience. Therefore, offering your books as a prize wouldn't be a good choice.

Instead, you need to choose something so compelling that people are really excited about it. Otherwise, they won't enter. And even if they do enter, they won't share the giveaway afterward, which means it won't go viral and you won't be able to significantly grow your email list.

Think of your target audience and try to understand what they might be interested in? If you write fantasy fiction, you might offer a multiple-author book bundle that consists of several popular books in this genre written by famous authors. Why would you want to advertise other authors' books? Because you need to reach their audience or, in this example - fantasy book readers. Apparently, if they love reading this genre, they might also be interested in your books.

Your prize needs to be related to your book and aimed at attracting your target audience. It doesn't have to be huge, but it should be attractive. Just make sure you offer something your target readers want to win. For example, if you write about graphic design, you might offer a graphic drawing tablet as a prize because that's something graphic designers may want to have.

You should choose a tangible product as the prize because it feels more valuable. Moreover, you won't be able to deliver eBooks without infringement of the other author's rights. Additionally, you should be ready to cover the shipping costs to deliver your prize to the winner.

An easy choice is to offer a Kindle book reader or an Amazon gift card. These are general gifts that many people may want to have, although only a few of them will be interested in your books. That's why you should be very specific with your giveaway prize because EVERYONE wants an

Amazon gift card or a Kindle reader, but you want to target only those people who belong to your target audience.

A good way to weed out those who are not interested in your books is to send them your Funnel Book or a reader magnet soon after they have entered your giveaway. Ask them to provide their email address (again) if they want to receive your book. Then leave only those who have done it on your list. That way, you will find out who actually is interested in your books. For example, if 5,000 people enter your giveaway, but only 2,000 of them download your Funnel Book afterward, keep only those 2,000 on your list and delete the others. It might feel painful, but it's necessary because you don't want to be sending emails to people that are not interested in your writing.

The most effective way to run your giveaways is by using a platform that is designed for it. Popular solutions are Rafflecopter, KingSumo, and Gleam. They help create well-designed giveaways in minutes. Features and pricing options vary, but the great thing about all these tools is that you have a lot more control over your campaign, and you can easily capture your audience's precious email addresses.

When you're writing your giveaway message, make sure that it includes a catchy headline. "Win 10 Children's Books!" is not as compelling as "Win 10 Educational Children's Books Worth $100." Keep your contest description short but tempting. Be sure to inform people that by entering your giveaway, they also agree to receive your marketing emails. If your giveaway platform does not make it clear that the entrant is simultaneously subscribing to additional promotional material, write it in your copy to avoid negativity.

Another important part of organizing your giveaway is advertising. It can make your giveaway go more viral but will also require a bigger budget. Invite your email list to participate in the giveaway and share it on social media to get additional reach and help it go wide and far. Promote it across all social media platforms that you have profiles on. Consider doing paid advertising on Facebook and Instagram. It will increase your campaign costs, but there is no point in spending money on prizes if you cannot reach a wide audience and get significant results. You need to do your planning and budgeting carefully. If you are not sure how to do Facebook ads effectively, there are many great online courses on Udemy.

You can organize your giveaway either individually or in a partnership with other authors in your genre. If you do it individually, you have all the control over its content and marketing. The downside is that it will be more difficult to reach a wide audience, and it will be more expensive because you will have to cover all the costs yourself. However, I recommend that you first try to do it on your own to learn the ropes before you involve other participants.

If you want to organize a joint giveaway with other authors, you will need to devote your time to find partners who are ready to share the expenses of the prize and advertising, if you do any. It means you need to know your budget before you contact anybody. The advantage of joint giveaways is you will have better chances to reach a huge audience. The disadvantage is that usually, in order to enter the giveaway, the reader must agree to subscribe to ALL the authors' newsletters in the promo. It means they can easily be overwhelmed by the email campaigns of all authors.

Let's assume you are doing a giveaway with ten authors. As soon as somebody subscribes to win the prize, they start receiving email campaigns from ten authors, and that may be so annoying that they unsubscribe from all or most of them. Still, joint giveaways can be one of the most effective ways to grow your readership super-fast.

In conclusion, experiment with all three promotion types described in this book and choose what works best for you. Be consistent and do at least one promotion each month to expose yourself to new potential readers because the more often you can reach a new audience, the quicker you will grow your mailing list.

Plan Your Email Content Calendar

Before you start collecting emails and working on creating your email campaigns, answer this question "What's the goal of growing your mailing list?" Why are you spending your time, energy, and probably money to have more email subscribers?

To be honest, my goal is to sell my books and earn income from affiliate sales. Your goal might be different, and this is perfectly fine. We can still be friends. However, I think that if you're spending so much time writing your books, creating reader magnets, and doing promotions to attract more subscribers, you should try to monetize your list by promoting your books and other products or services.

A study done by the Association of Sales Executives revealed that 81 percent of all sales happen on or after the fifth contact, which means that you should regularly communicate with your fans either by using automated email sequences or sending out broadcast emails. If you use your email list just for your book launches once a year, readers will forget who you are and move on to other authors who keep in touch with them regularly.

In general, there are two main marketing email types — **sequences and broadcasts**.

Email broadcast is **a one-time email campaign** that you manually send to your entire list or to a group of your contacts. Examples are time-sensitive sales and discounts, newsletters, updates, and digests. Usually, you send an email broadcast once, and that's it.

Email sequences **are a series of emails** that are automatically sent from your email marketing software based on your pre-defined time intervals or triggers (or both). In some cases (like transactional emails), the sequence is a single message. In other cases, a sequence may have tens of emails separated by scheduled delays. The beauty of the email sequences is that by implementing them, you're putting your email marketing on autopilot.

When you are working on your email content calendar, you should consider both email types.

Nurture Your Readers with Automated Email Sequences

Imagine every subscriber going through an email sequence that leads to your best and most relevant content and selling books while you are sleeping, having holidays, or writing! Wouldn't that be great?

Look, if you're not using automated emails to welcome, educate, nurture, and build relationships with your subscribers, you're shooting yourself in the foot! Not only are you missing out on building your author brand, connecting with your fans, and having more sales, but you're also doing your readers a huge disservice by not giving them the content they were looking for when they signed up. No matter whether these were educational tips or entertaining fiction stories, or discounts.

Let's look at the two types of email sequences.
- A time-based email sequence involves messages that are sent at predetermined intervals (for example, immediately after opt-in, five days after book download, two days after the previous email was opened, etc.).
- Trigger-based email sequences are sent whenever someone takes an action on your website or within your email sequence (for example, subscribes to your email list, clicks a link in an email, adds a product to the cart, etc.).

When you use both timed and trigger-based emails, they can move people through a journey of not having ever heard of you to becoming a paying reader and (potentially) an enthusiastic reviewer. Email sequences can deepen the relationships you have with your subscribers over time, solely through the content they share.

It doesn't matter if you write fiction or nonfiction; almost every author can benefit from email sequences. Whether you're using email to build your author brand, get leads, or drive traffic to your books, there's a sequence out there that can help you achieve your goals.

Welcome Email Sequence

Think, how you welcome new email subscribers to your list? Have you set up a simple autoresponder that says, "Thanks for signing up, here's your freebie," and then forget about them until when you want to sell them something? Or, are you treating every new subscriber like a VIP and sending automated value bombs in their inbox every few days after signup?

In short, a welcome email is your first introductory email that a reader gets when he or she subscribes to your email list. Its job is to make a good first impression of you as a brand, set the tone, and help you bond with your new audience. Subscribers are most engaged when they first sign up; therefore, welcome emails are one of the most effective automated emails and often have click-through rates that are about five times higher than those of regular broadcast emails.

A welcome email series is an automated email sequence that nurtures your new subscribers and leads them through small micro-commitments (such as reading a blog, completing a survey, watching a video, subscribing to your YouTube channel, etc.) with the goal of converting them to paying customers and loyal readers.

What should go into your welcome email series?

Honestly, it really depends on your niche and genre, the books and products you already have, and what actions you want the receivers to take. However, before you start writing your welcome email series, ask yourself one question – what do you want your subscribers to do at the end of the welcome series? What's the goal of the communication you are doing?

Your end goal could be to sell the next book in the series or even the entire series. Maybe you have an online course to offer or an affiliate product to suggest. Just keep in mind that the content you send to your new subscribers must be relevant to the source they came from. For example, if they subscribed for your romance novella reader magnet, the welcome series must be related to the romance novella genre and your other books in this sequel. But if they signed up for dog training tips, they should be welcomed with books and articles that are useful for dog owners.

If you don't have a product or service to sell yet, that's also OK. It's a wise move to start building your email list even before you create a product. In this case, highlight your brand and your best content (blog posts, videos, podcast, etc.).

In fact, the possibilities and combinations are endless. You decide what pathway might be the most beneficial to you and your readers.

For example, a simple welcome sequence could go like this:
- **Email 1:** Thanks for signing up, download your gift (include the link and directions to download your reader magnet). Tell readers about yourself, what content you share, and how frequently they

should emails expect from you. If you've been featured on high profile sites or podcasts, this is also your chance to let your new subscriber know about it. Show them you are a reliable source of information and author of good-quality books. Open a curiosity loop by promising valuable or entertaining content in the next email. For example, add a P.S. with a question: "Do you know that 58% of your audience will stop watching your video within the first 90 seconds? Would you like to know how to improve your video watch time? Then look out for my email tomorrow." However, be careful! Having too much information in a welcome email can get overwhelming.

- **Email 2:** Close the loop as promised in your first email. If you promised tips for improving video watch time, give them. Ask subscribers to tell you more about themselves by filling a survey if you write nonfiction. If you write fiction books, encourage them to reply to your message and tell you what kind of books they love to read, who their favorite authors are, etc. That way, you will have valuable information about your audience when you create your products and marketing messages.

- **Email 3:** If you have other relevant free books or reader magnets, send the download links to your subscribers without requesting them to opt-in with their emails again. Therefore, you will build on their feeling on reciprocity plus avoid duplicate contacts in your mailing list. Make sure all these resources link to your other books and products.

- **Email 4:** Promote the next (paid) book or the entire series. This is your time to sell. Be clear on why they should buy your book now, for example, because of the promotion or to achieve results faster. They have showed interest in your reader magnet, so it makes sense to tell them what else you have available.

- **Email 5:** Remind your subscribers about your other products and resources. For example, you can create a page with all your favorite tools and resources (including affiliate products) and link to this page. Look at my Tools page to get the idea: https://www.digginet.com/tools. That way, you will both provide valuable information and remind them about your products without being salesy.
- **Email 6:** Invite them to follow you on social media, Amazon, BookBub, and other profiles you have.

The main idea behind welcome email series is to encourage engagement and feedback. You want to introduce yourself and get to know your readers better. As a positive side effect, you will train them to open and respond to your emails.

Welcome emails usually go out every day. If it makes sense, you can also send out the first three emails each day and space out the rest in a week period. It depends on the content and call to actions you are using in your emails. Just ensure that subscribers do not receive the same welcome email sequence multiple times. This could happen if they sign up for another freebie that is linked to the same email sequence. For example, GetResponse provides functionality to set up sending automated emails only to unique recipients.

It's OK to start by having a general welcome email series. Over time, as you get more experience and your audience grows, you can become clearer and more targeted. Simply create the first sequence, launch it, and analyze the results. Look at the email open rates and click-through rates to understand which email campaigns work better or worse than others and where you have dropouts. Test different subject lines to see if the open rates improve. Also, refine the email copy and check if you can get better click-through rates.

Reviewer Sequence

Your biggest fans and readers are a tremendous resource and often undervalued. You can use their goodwill to promote your author brand and bring in new sales.

Create a list of your most active, engaging fans that have downloaded your Funnel Book and reader magnets. Some email marketing providers, like GetResponse, have a scoring system for each subscriber, allowing you to tell who your most engaged members are. Create a system where you regularly identify these engaged subscribers by tagging them. These are your fans who are the most likely to support you.

Then create a sequence of emails that encourages them to submit reviews on Amazon and other bookstores or share your content on social media. These people love your writing and voice, so they would be happy to contribute.

For example, after five days of downloading your free book, ask how the book is reading and if they want to share comments or suggestions on its content. That way, you will get valuable insights into your readers' minds and ideas for improvements and other content. Then after seven more days, ask if they have finished the book and would like to leave a review on Amazon.

You can easily combine the reviewer sequence with the welcome email sequence by making it a natural continuation of the conversation.

Launch Team Sequence

You need to build your launch team when you are about to launch your next book. Why do you need it? Because you will give them an advance review copy of your book so that they can read through it and write an honest review on Amazon when the book goes live. Amazon favors books with a good review activity. The more reviews your book receives during the launch period and later, the better they impact their sales and increase the possibility of getting promoted by Amazon in various lists and sections. Reviews are social proof that your book is being read and people are giving a high value to the content.

I'm not going to cover all the aspects of a successful book launch and recruiting your launch team members, because I've already explained this in my book, "Book Launch Formula: 3 Proven Strategies to Launch Your Nonfiction Book."But I'll give you an idea of the email sequence you should build to automatically communicate with your supporters.

Usually, you would need up to 10 emails within 2-3 weeks of the book launch period.

Here is a breakdown of the email sequence:
Email 1: Welcome them to the team and provide links to the PDF file of your book, for example, on BookFunnel, OneDrive, GoogleDrive, DropBox, or another similar platform. People must be able to download your book without having to sign up for an account.

Email 2: How is the book reading? Remind them about the general overview of the launch plan and the deadlines. Encourage them to send personal feedback and suggestions for improving your book.

Email 3: 5 Days Before Launch. Inform them when your book is going to be available on Amazon so that they can leave a review.

Email 4: The day before launch—Are you ready?

Email 5: LAUNCH DAY! It is time to download the book on Amazon and leave a review.

Email 6: Review reminder, updates on book status, and current ranking. Ask them to spread the word by sharing your social media posts about the book launch.

Email 7: Thank you for participating in the launch team and final update on the book's status.

In order to make the most of your launch team, be consistent in communicating with them. Long gaps in between emails will make people lose interest. **One email every 2-3 days would be a good regularity**. Make sure your team knows what to do and when to do it. Lead them by sending updates and informing them about the next actions to take. Prepare ahead of time and set up your book launch for success.

Re-engagement Sequence

Did you know that an email list naturally degrades by about 22.5% every year? It means if your list consists of 1,000 subscribers, only about 780 of them may still be active in one year. That's because contacts' email addresses change as they move from one email service provider to another and subscribers opt-out of your email communications.

There are two main disadvantages of having inactive contacts on your list:

1. The higher the number of inactive subscribers you have, the lower your open rates and other email marketing metrics. That's because you are mailing to inactive inboxes and readers. Even if your contacts remain subscribed, they may fall out of touch and become inactive and therefore skew your analytics and hurt your deliverability, engagement, and, as a result, your overall email marketing effectiveness.
2. All email delivery providers give you a sender score. The lower your opens and click-throughs, the lower your sender reputation and the higher the chances of your emails being flagged and delivered in the promotions or junk folder.

This is the reason why email list cleaning is so important. By removing the invalid, abandoned, or fake emails, you will prevent unnecessary damage to your reputation. Moreover, you won't keep paying for those unengaged subscribers on your list.

Email list subscribers become disengaged for many reasons -no matter how many nurturing sequences you have in place. It may be that their inboxes are flooded or they're no longer in the market for what you offer. It may also be that they simply don't find value in your emails anymore because their interests have changed.

Whatever their reason, you should still do your best to renew the relationship and remind them about the value you could give before you remove them. Re-engagement sequences work perfectly for this goal and could be set up as an automation that is triggered after a subscriber has been inactive for a certain period of time, say 90 days.

For example, you might define a subscriber who hasn't opened any of your emails for 90 days as inactive. Once an account becomes inactive, the re-engagement sequence sends out emails designed to get the subscriber to interact with you (maybe with a quiz, special offer, or bonus). If they don't respond, send an email with a straightforward question, like, "Am I still welcome in your inbox?" Include a link to your page and ask them to click on it if they still want to receive emails in the future. You will track those clicks in your email marketing platform later.

A simple re-engagement sequence could go like this:
Email 1: An incentive or some kind of interactive content to engage inactive subscribers.
Email 2: Am I still welcome in your inbox? Ask them to click on your link to prove they want to stay on your list.

Email 3: Is this goodbye? (sent to those inactive subscribers that didn't open the previous emails)

After one week (to give them time to read your email), it's time for the final step – delete those inactive subscribers who didn't click on the link in your emails. I know it's gut-wrenching to delete those hard-earned subscribers, but it will be worth it because your open rates and engagement rates will increase. If you don't clean your list at least every three months, then you are wasting your money on hosting inactive contacts. Yes, you should clear your list four times a year. Every quarter.

Eliminate invalid addresses and inactive contacts because it's much better to have a smaller, engaged list than a large and unresponsive one. Moreover, if you have an active and good quality email list, you get a more precise reflection of what content and email subject lines resonate with your audience.

To wrap it up, I know that creating all these email sequences takes a lot of time and work, and that may feel overwhelming. However, I think that before you even launch your email list (start collecting email addresses), you need to have at least a basic system in place. Start with your welcome email sequence, then move on to the reviewers' sequence. If you are going to launch a book, make sure you have your launch team email sequence ready. Continue analyzing your subscriber data and building additional nurturing sequences. The good news is, once you build them, they won't take so much of your time anymore. Sure, you will need to revise the sequences periodically, say every 3 months, to make sure they are still relevant, but it's not going to be so time-consuming anymore.

Broadcast emails

Why would you need to send broadcast emails if you are already using automated email sequences? Because email sequences, in many cases, are evergreen (not time-related), but broadcast emails are used to deliver time-sensitive information. They inform about discounts, free promotions, and book launches.
How often should you send your broadcast email campaigns? If you ask three email marketing experts this question, you will get three different answers.

My answer is: it depends on your goals. Do you have books or courses to sell? Do you regularly do cross-promotions, joint promotions, or giveaways? Do you write a blog? Do you have an email strategy around your critical business dates or national holidays? If yes, you already have an idea of what topics you could cover in your emails and how often you should communicate with your audience.

Moreover, consider this: if you're not promoting at least two paid products a month to your email list, then you are under-monetizing a highly-valuable sales channel. You can promote your books, online courses, services, affiliate products, or other items. Usually, subscribers will buy your products much more willingly than they will ever buy a product you endorse. However, considering the low profit you can make by selling books on Amazon, it's also a good idea to promote higher ticket affiliate products to additionally monetize your list and earn extra income. Otherwise, you are leaving a lot money on the table. It might be more difficult for fiction writers to find appropriate affiliate products; however, you can still play with price discounts and do cross-promotions.

Rather than trying to figure out what to write in your broadcast emails, create a monthly email content plan with deadlines. These can be two emails a week or more. Having a plan ensures you stay consistent and move toward your goal. A simple list of email topics and send date might be enough. It doesn't have to be complicated –at least in the beginning. The main thing here is to be consistent and keep in touch with your subscribers regularly, instead of only knocking on their door when you need something.

Plan your email content calendar around your chosen offers and promotions to warm up your readers at least 2-3 weeks ahead so that they have all the information they need to say YES to your offer when it's time. For instance, if you have an affiliate promotion for a dog trick training course on September 15, send emails about trick training advantages to pre-sell the idea and move the email readers closer to the decision to buy the course when you announce it.

The good news is, once you create emails that promote your content and books, you can create an automated sequence made of them. It means you can gradually add more and more emails to your sequences to make sure every new subscriber gets the links to your best content. One of my sequences has grown over the years and currently consists of 26 emails. It means I can spend months without worrying about writing emails. The automated email sequences are, in my opinion, the easiest way to sell books while you sleep. They run in the background non-stop and send your emails when you tell them to.

Here are a few different types of emails you can send as broadcast emails and later transform into an automated sequence:

- Answer a commonly asked question
- Link to cornerstone pieces on your blog
- Share your favorite tool collection like in this example: https://www.digginet.com/tools
- Bust a myth that your subscribers may think is true
- Request to fill your survey
- Tell a case study about how you achieved a specific result
- Show a behind-the-scenes look into your writing journey
- Ask your subscribers to fill an entertaining quiz

Feel free to "borrow" other great ideas from the gurus in your niche. Simply subscribe to their email lists and see what information they send to you. Pay special attention to the first 5-7 emails you get to understand their welcome email sequences. Read their subject lines and emails, click the links, and check what products they are promoting. Figure out similar or better things you could do. Don't copy. Get inspired and write your own emails using their best examples.

Some people don't want to "be annoying" by emailing too often. In this case, experiment to find out what works best for you. But consider this – your subscribers have subscribed to your list to receive emails from you.

In case they're not comfortable with your email frequency, they can easily unsubscribe. You shouldn't feel bad about it because if they unsubscribe, they are not loyal to you. Not all unsubscribes are bad. The larger your mailing list, the more you need to pay for using your email marketing platform. If they unsubscribe, they free up space for new subscribers who may be much more loyal and engaged with your content. Moreover, if you don't communicate with your email list, why do you need it at all?

You shouldn't worry about sending emails to people who have agreed to receive emails from you. On any given day, I get multiple emails from big companies. Most of them are hard sales emails. I doubt they are concerned about a few unsubscribes. Actually, having a 0.5% unsubscribe rate is absolutely normal. However, you might need to reconsider your email frequency and content when the rate is higher than that.

Still, I don't think that every email you send should be a "buy-my-stuff" email. A good rule of thumb is that only one-third of your communication should be hard push sales emails. The rest should be educational or entertaining content to mix things up.

Segment Your Email List

What you need to realize is that your email list subscribers are not all the same. While some of them have been receiving your emails for years, others may be very new to your list. Moreover, if you offer various ways for people to subscribe to your list (multiple Funnel Books, reader magnets, and opt-in forms), make sure that you have no holes and that every subscriber is getting targeted information no matter how they come into your system. In order to do that, you need to set a clear pathway every subscriber takes before, when, and after they join your email list.

What do I mean by that?

In short, EVERY freebie or reader magnet you offer must have:
- A subscription form (either embedded in a landing page or free-standing as a banner or pop-up on your web page).
- An automated welcome email sequence of about 1-5 emails.
- A tagging and segmentation system in place so that you can create personalized and targeted communication later.

Why do you need these? Rather than sending the same marketing messages to all your contacts, having a segmented list helps you create and send more relevant content that is based on particular interests and behaviors of your readers. Therefore, you will not annoy your subscribers with irrelevant information. This is especially important if you have a variety of offerings that are targeted to different audiences.

For example, my mailing list is divided into those who are interested in self-publishing and those who are interested in creating marketing content in general. While some topics might be relevant for both audiences (for example, productivity tools), it's clear that not all my subscribers will be interested in launching a book on Amazon.

There are several ways you can find out your subscribers' interests:

- **Your Funnel Book and reader magnets.** If a reader opts-in for a freebie (for example, on book cover design), they are raising their hand and indicating that this is something they are interested in. They probably need help to improve in that area. If you nurture them, build trust, show your expertise, and then try to sell them an online course on book cover design principles, they are more likely to buy it as opposed to if you pitch them something on logo design. It means all your lead magnets must lead subscribers somewhere and be aligned with your existing or future offers to position you as an expert or authority on the topic you want to be known for. In case you have reader magnets that don't correspond to this rule, you should consider getting rid of them because they are almost useless. Even if they convert well, you will gather an audience that is not really interested in your paid products.

    If you are a fiction writer, use your freebies to introduce and upsell your book sequels. In case you write in a different genre (for example, romance and horror), make sure you have different funnel books and reader magnets for each of them. That way, every time you write an email to your readers, you will be able to adjust your voice, email content, and other book offers according to the readers' preferences.

- **Emails they open and links they click.** Every email marketing software provides functionality that lets you see which subscribers have opened your emails and clicked on the links. If you write books about dog training (sorry, dogs again...) and invite your readers to visit a blog post about puppy potty training, you can easily segment out those who are interested in this topic just by analyzing their behavior. If people have opened your message with a subject line that clearly states, "7 Tips for Puppy Potty Training", and even followed the link in your message to read the blog post, most probably that's because they already have a puppy or are going to have one in the nearest future. That way, you can easily predict the interest in your paid products.

- **2-Question Surveys.** Ask your contacts about their challenges when they sign up or send out an online survey to your existing contacts. Don't create a long survey. 1-2 questions are enough. For example, if you assume that all contacts that opt-in for a particular reader magnet are dog owners, you can ask them if they belong to one of these segments: a) an aspiring dog owner; b) a puppy owner; c) an adult dog owner. That way, you can get an insight **into what stage** of owning a dog they are in and get an idea of what challenges they may have. It's also advisable to ask one open-ended question in your survey **to understand their pain points**. The question is, "What's your main struggle when it comes to (...your topic...)?". This question is widely used in marketing, and maybe you have already heard about it or even answered it. Depending on how you structure your question, you can get a lot of insight into the interests of your subscribers and readers. Doing a survey like this is a great way to understand what words and sentences your target audience uses to describe their pain points. Then you can use these expressions when writing your landing page copy and book blurbs. That way, your target audience will recognize and identify with the problem, and your offer also will become more attractive.

Luckily, you don't have to use fancy and expensive tools to create your small survey. Google Forms is a simple yet effective tool for creating a basic survey like this: https://forms.gle/fu3oF7nirujaYdeK7. Place your survey in the thank you page of your reader magnet to instantly get feedback from your subscribers while they are most interested in connecting with you. Additionally, include it as a link in your welcome email and periodically send it out to your list to gather more data.

How to Group Your Contacts?

In general, you can group your contacts into different lists and add tags to categorize them even further for targeted and personalized email campaigns. If your email marketing software provides contact scoring according to the receivers' engagement rate (frequency of email opens, link clicks, downloads, and purchases), you can also segment them using this criterion to create special promotions for your most active contacts and reactivation campaigns for the inactive ones.

As a book author, you might find it useful to group reader magnets, website content, and email sequences according to your book topics or genre. This means that you should have different sequences for each topic or book sequel. When you're starting out, it may be fairly straightforward because you may not have many reader magnets and books. However, as you write more books on different topics and create more reader magnets, it may get complicated. Therefore, having a good foundation and system in place is very important right from the start so that you don't accidentally leave out a group of subscribers from receiving your welcome emails and topic-related content.

Let's look at the difference between email list segmentation and tagging and how you can put these features to use in your own email marketing.

Email Lists

When a new contact fills the subscription form, their email address lands in the list linked to this form. If you have done everything right, the moment that happens, you know that they are interested in the topic your freebie represents, or they have chosen to sign up. That's the first step in your email list segmentation.

If you write both fiction and nonfiction, but the person subscribes only for your nonfiction content, it's clear they are not really interested in your fiction books and wouldn't be bothered about them. But if you write about dog training and they download all three reader magnets that talk about different aspects of this topic, you can be very sure they are interested in raising a dog.

Considering the examples above, every time you want to inform your subscribers about your fiction book promos, you send email campaigns to the list that consists of your fiction readers. But if you want to send useful content about your non-fiction topics, you choose your other list.

The fun starts when you have many reader magnets about similar topics and multiple lists because it gets much more difficult to segment out those contacts who might be interested in your email subject and build email automations with useful content. This is when contact tagging comes into play.

Tagging

In general, a tag is a particular label or keyword you attach to a contact to identify or categorize it. For example, every time somebody downloads my Funnel Book, "5 Secret Strategies of Kindle Publishing: Earn Passive Income with Nonfiction Books," GetResponse (the app I use) adds the "self-publishing" tag to this contact. The same tag is also added to those contacts that have downloaded reader magnets that are related to other self-publishing topics. That way, if at some point I want to make a list of all those subscribers that are interested in book publishing, I can easily do that with just a few clicks.

Tags allow you to classify your contacts. While email lists are groups of people you repeatedly want to email, tags allow you to save additional information about your contacts, so you can send emails to an even more targeted group when necessary. The good news is, you can tag contacts automatically at different stages of their lifecycle.

However, before you start tagging your list, you need to decide what you'd like to use tags for. Because if you create too many different tags, you'll end up with a mess. First, think about what actions or behaviors might warrant a tag, as well as how these tags could be useful to you.

Let's look at the most popular tags!

- Source tag – used to track where your contacts originated from, for example, source – joint promotion, Funnel Book download, etc.
- Trigger tag – used to initiate processes by triggering an action. Trigger tags typically begin automations with the "Tag is added" and "Tag is removed" start triggers. For example, every time my subscriber gets tagged with "self-publishing," they start receiving an automated email sequence on related topics.
- Product tag – indicates which product a contact has purchased, for example – eBooks, courses, or others). For example, with **GetResponse** you can create simple sales funnels to sell your digital products independently from Amazon. If you use their system, every time somebody buys a product, they will be assigned a tag that will help you segment out paying customers from freebie seekers. Additionally, an abandoned cart tag will identify those who visited your sales page but didn't buy. Thanks to the tagging system, you can send reminder email (abandoned cart) campaigns to these contacts.
- Action tag – describes any kind of contact behavior, for example: downloaded an eBook, left a review on Amazon.

Tags to your contacts can be added either automatically or manually. It's not possible to automatically track which of your book launch team members have actually left reviews on Amazon. But if they tell you they did, you can go to their contact cart and manually add the tag. That way, you will know who your most loyal and committed launch team members are. Then you can work on engaging with them even more by creating a VIP team and building relationships so that they stay loyal in the future.

The Art of Writing Catchy Subject Lines

The subject of an email is like the title of a book. It must entice your reader to open your email and start reading. Otherwise, your email can literally go unnoticed, or even worse head straight to the trash. If no one opens your email, you cannot benefit from your mailing list in any way – no clicks, no downloads, no sales. I have experimented with different subject lines for the same email and have seen that open rates can increase from 21 - 43% just by changing the subject line alone. This is how powerful they can be.

Writing great subject lines is a part of the copywriting art, which is not really the topic of this book; however, I feel like I cannot entirely skip this topic. Therefore, in this chapter, I'll give you a few ideas for crafting effective email subject lines.

1. **Keep it short and sweet**

Use no more than 9 words and 60 characters for your subject line if you want it to be easily readable on mobile devices because about 61.9% of email opens usually occur on mobile. Since phone screens are small, it's more difficult to read long subject lines. Think about which words matter less and remove all unnecessary details.

2. **Add humor**

Funny subject lines never disappoint. You never know; you may be adding a smile to a sad soul with your humor. A humorous subject line motivates the reader to open the mail. However, you have to ensure it is well placed and not offensive in any way. Keep in mind that something funny to you may irritate someone else. So, know your audience well: their gender, cultural life, and what they like. Having such information will help you use the perfect phrase that'll make them laugh. But don't focus so much on making the reader crack a rib and forget to bring out the main information. Take it as a powerful tool for marketing, and not a mission of making the reader have the loudest laughter. Examples are:

- Why your cat knows more about marketing than you
- Do or die

3. Shock with strange statements

Ever saw a horrifying notification pop out on your phone and you were not able to look away? It's difficult to ignore such notices. Your audience, too, will be unable to resist your email if you use a shocking subject line. The reader will be eager to discover more about this scary information you want to share. Still, the news must be relevant and shouldn't be insulting to anyone. Examples are:

- Let's get married
- Only one human left on this planet

4. Use numbers

Using numeric in your subject line is a great way of gaining the mind's focus. Numbers stand out and break the reading boredom significantly. Let's be real here. If you see two headlines – '5 ways to become rich' and 'how to get rich– which will you go for? There is no doubt that only a few will go for the latter. The first one is clear and direct to the point. I'll think

I only have five points to read, but I'll probably think the second option has larger information, which I don't have time for. Many people may reason like me. Your subject line will stand out more if you use this approach, and you'll have more clicks than a sender who doesn't use it.

For example:
- 3 secrets for a happy marriage life
- The top 5 under $10

5. Show personalization

Let's face it. We often ignore messages from sources we are not familiar with. So, subject lines that imply the sender knows who you are can be a real kick in getting the receiver's attention. However, adding the user's name in the subject line has been misused and is no longer as effective as before. Extend your creativity by addressing the receiver by acknowledging any personal detail. You can mention their location or the things they love.

Here are some examples:
- The unknown facts about your favorite author
- How to be a better mother

6. Challenge the reader

Question marks challenge the readers. The questions get them into thinking and make them want to confirm any added information on top of what they already know. They'll feel engaged and always look forward to your next email to see what you have for them. Use strange punctuation marks to win the jackpot. Look for catchy symbols but be careful not to create an impression that the email is spam. You'll get more results if the questions are emotionally engaging. You can try:

- Is this why you are failing?
- It's weekend! #time to spoil yourself

7. Use the fear of missing out

An easy way to get people's attention is to make them feel like they might miss out on something important unless they act now. It's called FOMO or fear of missing out. This factor is often used in sales campaigns to emphasize that the decision must be taken now, or you will miss the good price and offer.

Here are some examples:

- [URGENT] Only one day left to get 50% off...
- Our sale ends in 24 hours

Experiment with different techniques to see what type of subject lines work best for you, your audience, and book sales. Personalize your emails, make sure they are relevant to your target audience, and use catchy and pleasant language. There are hundreds of great email subject lines on the internet. Just search on Google, and you will find long lists with ideas for almost any niche and occasion. Also check your inbox. Most probably, there are some creative examples there, too. Think which subject lines made you open emails and which did not. Try to model the ones that compelled you to click. Most probably, they will also stand out in your reader's inboxes. If you send an email to your subscribers and see a low open rate, wait for three days and change the subject line. Then send it again to all those who didn't open the previous email. You might be surprised by the results you get.

Measure Your Email Performance

If you are familiar with email marketing, then most probably you already know most of these metrics. Still, I'll list them here as a short reminder and reference for those of my readers who are just starting out because these are important statistics that you should be measuring regularly. The numbers are provided by every email marketing platform, so you don't need to worry about how to calculate them; however, it's good to understand the principles behind them. If you don't track your numbers, you cannot analyze your email marketing performance. You won't know if something worked or not, and therefore, you won't know if you should do it again or move on to something else.

1. Open Rate
Email open rate is the percentage of email recipients who opened your email. This is an important metric that can be directly influenced by writing catchy subject lines. We already touched on this topic in the previous chapter. However, one more factor that can influence the open rate is the email sender's name. Actually, that's even the more important factor.

Think about it for a moment. If you receive two emails – one is from me and the other from your mother. Which one will you open first? I guess it will be your mom's email and no matter what the subject line is. Similarly, it works with brands. Most probably, you prefer one brand over another, which means that you will open emails from your preferred brand more often than those from brands that you don't like or trust. What can you do about that? Work on your reputation and brand (e.g., author name) recognition. Offer good quality content in your emails so that people associate them with something valuable and worth reading.

How to Calculate: Total Opens/ Emails Delivered
When to Track: Weekly

2. Click-Through Rate (CTR)

Click-through rate is the percentage of email recipients who clicked on a link or call to action button inside your email. This is often the main goal you want to achieve, because you want your readers to take action and go to your website, watch a video or check out your book on an online bookstore. Therefore, it's a very important metric to measure because it shows how many people actually followed your link. If you have a great open rate but no clicks, it's either your email copy doesn't do its job, or the content is irrelevant.

How to Calculate: Total Clicks / Total Emails Delivered
When to Track: Weekly

3.Click-to-open rate (CTOR)

Unlike click-through rate, click-to-open rate is the number of clicks **out of the number of unique opens** (instead of the number of delivered emails), and it measures the effectiveness of your email's content. In this case, only clicks by people that actually viewed your email are counted; therefore, this metric shows you how effective the email message was and whether it generated enough interest in the email reader to click on your links. Your CTOR is influenced by your copywriting skills, link text, as well as the link location in the body of your email, and the number of times you included the link.

How to Calculate: Unique Clicks / Unique opens
When to Track: Weekly

4. Unsubscribe Rate

Unsubscribe rate is the percentage of email recipients who clicked on the "unsubscribe" link inside your email. It can be influenced by many factors. Unsubscribe rates can be high if you don't email frequently enough and your sender's name isn't recognizable or has a low reputation. It can also be high when you don't have a strong welcome series, if you email too frequently, if you use misleading subject lines, and many other factors.

How to Calculate: Total Unsubscribes / Emails Delivered
When to Track: Weekly

5. Conversion Rate (CVR)

Conversion rate is the percentage of email recipients who completed your desired action (e.g., bought your book, filled a survey, signed up for a webinar, etc.). The number of subscribers that carry out your desired actions are called conversions. Usually, it's something that happens on your website after someone clicks on a link inside your email.

The problem is, unless you use UTM links or have other web user behavior tracking systems in place, you cannot precisely measure this metric. However, you can still have some idea about your email performance in terms of conversions. Let's say you send a promotional email to your subscribers with a call-to-action to buy your new book, but you don't see any sales. This means your conversion rate is zero. On the other hand, if the email campaign is successful, you may see some spike in sales on Amazon. Although you won't have precise numbers because the spike in sales can also be due to other factors, you can still have some idea of your email performance if you check the other email marketing metrics. You can get much more precise data on your conversion rate if you check affiliate links because they are trackable. In case you get ten affiliate sales after mailing about the product, you can easily calculate your conversion rate.

How to Calculate: Total Conversions / Emails Delivered
When to Track: Weekly

6. List Growth Rate

List growth rate is the metric to track the pace at which your list has grown over a certain period of time, for example, a week, a month or other periods. It's natural to experience some attrition, so focus on ways to continually grow your list, engage existing subscribers, and find new ones because if your list isn't growing, it's dying. Once you know your overall growth rate, look at sources that bring you new contacts and the contact quality. This will give insight into which sign-up forms, landing pages, and marketing channels work better for growing your list.

How to Calculate: New Subscribes − (Unsubscribes + Complaints + Bounces) / Total Subscribers

When to Track: Monthly

7.Open Reach

Open reach is the percentage of subscribers who opened at least ONE email during a specific period (for example, a month or a longer period). If the open rate is calculated on an individual email campaign basis, then it is calculated **over a series of emails** and measures your list's overall engagement.

Let's assume that your email list consists of 1,000 subscribers, and you sent four email campaigns to all of them during a month. That's 4,000 emails in total. The average open rate for these emails was 20%. That means each campaign was opened by 200 subscribers. However, you don't know if these are the same 200 people who typically open your emails every time or another 200 people. How many of your subscribers opened at least ONE of these four emails?

If your email campaign was opened every time by different 200 subscribers, your overall open reach would be 80%. Although it might sound unrealistic at the first moment, it can be easily achieved if every time you sent your email only to those subscribers that didn't open the previous one. That way, you can achieve that by the end of the month.

80% of your list will know about your offer! This is how powerful open reach can be.

How to Calculate: Unique Subscribers Who Open At least One Email / Unique Subscribers Who Received At least One Email

When to Track: Monthly

OK, now you are aware of the most important email marketing metrics you should be tracking. Let's take a look at the averages of different industries to benchmark your metrics and set realistic goals and measure your email performance: https://www.smartinsights.com/email-marketing/email-communications-strategy/statistics-sources-for-email-marketing. However, don't simply rely on the average numbers of the industry. The reported numbers include different business types and list sizes. Instead, set your own benchmarks by looking at the numbers for each of your email campaigns and their averages. If you send different email types (remember the email sequences chapter!), track metrics for each of them. This may include tracking your welcome email series, launch team email series, broadcast emails, and others. It's equally important to track your subscribers' engagement and run a data hygiene check regularly. Carrying out these two simple steps can help the overall success of your email marketing campaigns.

5 Questions to Answer Before Choosing Your Email Marketing Platform

When comparing different email marketing platforms to choose the one that would suit your needs, remember to think in the long-term. As your email list and product range grow, you will need more features and services to reach your income goals. If you create many opt-in forms, landing pages, and automated email sequences on one email marketing platform and then decide that this platform doesn't work for you anymore and want to migrate to another, it may be a difficult and time-consuming process. You will need to spend the time that you could devote to writing and marketing your books on doing boring and technical tasks.

That's why it's important to think in the long term and have a vision of what features and functionality you are going to need in the future. Answer the five questions below to have a better idea of the main things you need to consider when choosing your email marketing platform.

Can I create modern and good-looking email subscription forms and landing pages?

The first thing you need to find out is whether the email marketing platform provides options to create opt-in forms, pop-ups, and landing pages. Moreover, check out if these forms can be easily embedded and integrated into your webpage. Here is an example of one of my landing pages: https://5kindle-strategies.digginet.com. As you can see, it is a free-standing page that has no distractions, no click-away, and is created for one and only purpose – to get a conversion. Moreover, instead of some generic xyz.com domain, I'm using my brand sub-domain to increase visitors' trust.

My own favorite email marketing platform is GetResponse (most probably, you have already guessed that) because it has all the features to build good-looking landing pages with subscription forms, pop-ups for my webpage, sophisticated email automation sequence, and even simple lead generation and sales funnels like the one below that shows statistics for every step of my subscribers. Thanks to the illustration they provide, I can see the flow of my leads, starting from the number of visitors to the landing page to the number of subscribers that converted in the final step of my funnel.

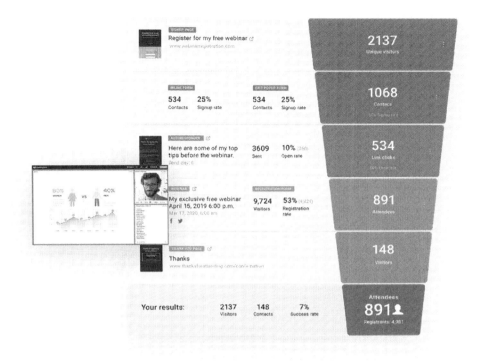

That way, I can easily see the weakest points in my lead magnet funnel and improve them to increase the conversion rate. For example, if I see that I drastically lose leads in the second or third step, I may decide to improve the texts or design of my landing page or emails. Or do some A/B tests. Anyway, it's good to see the whole picture to not rely on guesses.

Can I do different kinds of email campaigns with the system?

Once you've determined what email types you are going to create and send to your subscribers, you'll want to make sure your email marketing platform can actually do what you want. Find out if you'll be able to send not only simple broadcast emails but also automated email sequences, e.g., welcome email series, launch team series, and other trigger or event-based emails with special offers for customers interested in a specific topic or genre.

What's the personalization potential?

Personalized content that is targeted to specific segments can drastically improve your email marketing results – increase book sales, engagement, and number of reviews. By now, you should already know that email personalization goes far beyond using the customers' names in email subject lines. The key to personalization, in fact, rests more on what you know about the contacts on your list. Check out if your chosen email marketing platform provides options to tag, score, and segment your contacts based on their behavior – email opens, clicks, downloads, and preferences.

Can I build sales funnels and do marketing automation?

At some point in your email marketing journey, you may want to implement sophisticated automations, for example, prepare tailored emails based on your web page visits, send abandoned cart emails to encourage visitors to finish their purchases, automatically recommend books and other products based on the subscriber's purchase history. Even if it might sound like a distant future at the moment, it's still good to know you will be able to easily start using this functionality when you need it. That's why it's so important to make sure your email marketing platform is advanced enough to support your increasing needs.

Will the price be acceptable for you even when your list expands?

Let's face it; when you're just starting with a shoe-string budget, price is one of the most important factors that influence your decision. Thanks to the wide range of different solutions available, you can get started with an email marketing platform for as little as free or under $10 per month to something that costs a couple of hundred dollars monthly. However, it's very important to consider both price and features of the platform in the long run because as your list expands, you may want to do much more sophisticated things with your contacts.

Take my personal experience as an example. When I was just getting started on my list building journey, I started with MailChimp because I could use it for free. However, as my email list grew and I wanted to upgrade my account, I realized that this platform doesn't offer me some of the functionality I needed to level up my email marketing campaigns. Therefore, I had to spend a lot of my time to move all my contacts, subscription forms, and landing pages to another platform that was much more suitable for my goals. Believe me – it was a very time consuming, frustrating, and boring task.

Now it's your turn!

I'll be very short here. Stop reading and start doing because knowing and not doing is the same as not knowing. Take everything you learned in this book and put it into practice. Partner with authors in your niche or genre, grow your email list, create valuable content and automate your email sequences to spend less time on marketing and have more time for writing your books and building your presence on Amazon.

The best part about being a self-published author is the chance to try out different things for yourself. You don't have to believe me or anyone else. Simply try it yourself, look at the metrics, and make business decisions with numbers, not guesses or hopes. Your mailing list is your warmest audience. They signed up to hear from you. Use them and sell to them.

Hopefully, by now, you already have a vision of how to build your email marketing strategy. If you found my book helpful, please leave a review. Your review is very important because it will help other readers to decide if this book could be useful for them, too. It doesn't have to be a long paragraph. Just a line or two would mean a lot to me.

In case you want to be notified when I publish new books, **please** follow me on Amazon and subscribe to my readers' list here for a personal email from me: https://notification.digginet.com.

Useful Tools for Authors and Content Creators

I get asked all the time what tools and resources I use to self-publish my books and create content for social media. I have published a list of my favorite ones on my blog. Check them out here: https://www.digginet.com/tools.

Found a Typo?

Although I do my best to ensure that this book is flawless, it is inevitable that a mistake or two will get unnoticed.

If you find an error of any kind in this book, please let me know by sending an email to info@digginet.com. This will ensure that other readers will never have to experience that terrible typo. I appreciate your taking the time to notify me – you will make the world a better place.

Other Books by the Author

Sell Books on Amazon Series

- 5 Secret Strategies of Kindle Publishing: Earn Passive Income with Nonfiction Books
- Book Cover Design Formula: Create Book Covers That Captivate Readers
- Book Launch Formula: 3 Proven Strategies to Launch Your Nonfiction Book on Amazon
- Email Marketing for Authors Made Simple: The 1 Page List Building Plan
- Plan Out Your Nonfiction Book Series

Free Online Tools Series

- 100+ Free Online Tools to Get Things Done Quicker
- 100+ Free Tools to Create Content for Web & Social Media
- 200 Free Tools to Save Time on Social Media Managing: Boost Your Social Media Results & Reduce Your Hours

Be Your Own Designer Series

- How to Create a Logo? Fundamental Principles of Effective Logo Design
- Graphic Design for Beginners: Fundamental Graphic Design Principles that Underlie Every Design Project

About the Author

Anita Nipane is a two-times Amazon bestselling author and owner of the marketing blog www.digginet.com where she shares useful tips for content creators and self-published authors. With a Master's in Business Administration and numerous qualifications in marketing, Anita has a long experience as a marketing manager in different industries. In her books, Anita explains complex content creation matters in an easy-to-understand and structured way.

When she is not writing books or spending time with her horse, she is passionate about exploring the world, one awesome adventure at a time.

Made in the USA
Middletown, DE
17 March 2023